# All her Shades of Purple

Erica Da Silva

Presentation by *BookLeaf Publishing*

Web: www.bookleafpub.com

E-mail: info@bookleafpub.com

ISBN: 9789357212090

First edition 2023

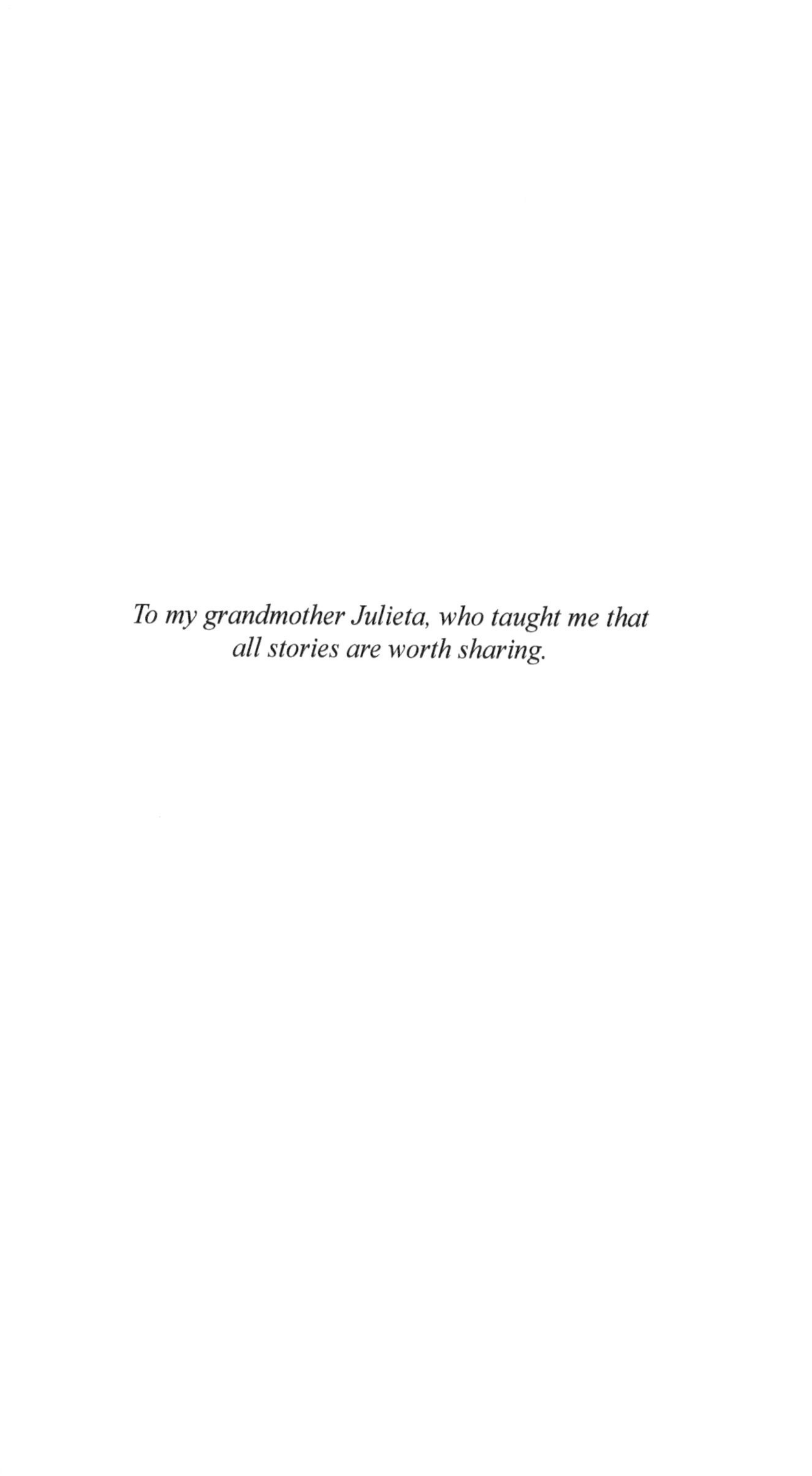

*To my grandmother Julieta, who taught me that
all stories are worth sharing.*

# ACKNOWLEDGEMENT

Embarking on a 21 day writing challenge sounds easy enough but many were the moments where I thought I would not see its end.
A big thank you to my little sister Mafalda, who spent evenings brainstorming a thousand memories of our grandmother with me and helping me finish many of these poems.

A thank you also to my loving partner, who sat with me on the last day of the challenge working through my last poem and offering a clear perspective. Your love and support are essential, always.

Thank you to my mother and all those who keep grandma's memories alive.

And finally, thank you to my fluffy boy, Milo, your dog cuddles and kisses make every day better.

# The Pearl

Island of eternal spring
Where from deepest blue a mountain rose
And red flames the skies enclosed
From ash and grief this place was born
Once a lost tear, now an eternal pearl.

Island of eternal sunshine
Unending sky, countless stars
A garden of dreams where hopes will grow
Secrets exposed through its petals, now are
known.

Island of sorrow
As told by Silvester's song
Once a lost tear, now an eternal pearl.
Oh don't let it sink in your grieving heart
Now its land is a safe home, where our story
shall start.

Island, her home, her prideful land
In here she grew, she loved, she danced
In here she flew,
And held your hand.

# 1933

The year of 1933
Is a special year for me.
A torch lit up this world alone
Whose light would forever fill my home.

The year of 1933
For many was filled with glee
Almost
In a blizzard of silence
A powerful movement rose
But not yet, they said, you need to read more
books,
Not simply read and write
To earn such right.

The year of 1933
When no one but she was born
Into a family of 4
But only 3 would live on.

The year of 1933
Is a year I speak of proudly,
There she was born in an island
That would come to know her well.

The year of 1933
Are you still with me?
For all the things that took place then,
I pray Amen, Amen, Amen
For this was when she came to be.

# Working is for men

Working is for men
They used to say back then
But you were barely 17
Still young and so green.

The land was not enough
But any other path would be too tough
Still, you bravely went, studied and  learnt
Then suddenly, you had earned
The respect that in a small island
Women earned by being silent.

You worked so hard, needle and thimble
Years of practice made you nimble
And still today they all admire
What became your art, your passion, your fire.

Working is for men,
They used to say back then
But women worked with all their body
And each scar could tell a story

Working is for men,
They used to say back then,
But to this day I have to meet
A man whose art burns so deep.

# If you shall marry

If you shall marry
And marry you will
Do it wisely, carefully, under God's will
Know that marriage is for life
And I want you to walk that path

But if you shall marry,
I know you will
Do it once I am not here
Hold on still

For if you marry
And when you do
When it goes wrong
And I can't be there for you
To watch you suffer under a man's grip
I couldn't bear to watch you
Forever his ownership

So listen to your mother girls,
When you marry
Do it when I'm gone.
For I would rather not mourn
Because divorce is not a choice.

And just like this, again and again
Her mother's words would echo in her brain
During those long hours when alone she would sigh
Afraid of what the night would bring to her side.
No, later she would think,
No to his grip, no to ownership
For I did wait and somehow you knew
That things would go wrong
Bruised, purple and blue
But I said No
And  I would say it earlier
Even despite what I was taught
I said No
And I would say it again.

# Death of a Mother

I have been told long ago,
That it was you who dressed her up,
Brushed her hair, unknotted her curls
Untangled her rings from her frozen fingers
Like lost treasures kept from the coffin.

You never told me of such pain
Of losing your mother and of caring for death
Of washing her cold body and laying her to rest
You never told me grandma, of such pain
Of laying her down never to see her again
Of not having her near you when life became
brutal.

You never told me of such pain
Because when I remember you today
I think of your laugh, your light, your glow
Oh grandma but it must have hurt you
Even when joy was always on show.

# Olive Tree

When your name connotes to nature
But you want to keep her from growing
Just remember that like trees
People's wings will keep showing.

Oh what have you done to our nation
Many say you restored us all
Like a saviour, Salazar
Keeping us from the fall.

Grandma, you told me about him
Forgotten by some, remembered by many
Antonio de Oliveira Salazar,
But statues there aren't any.

A man who drank the Portuguese freedom
Like Portuguese men drink their wine
He was among many of the stories you told me
And so it goes the storyline

Salazar a man who rose to power,
When you weren't even a little girl
Freedom suddenly became hidden
The outrage rising, in a swirl

Although his name connotes to nature, you said
An Olive tree growing in our land
All trees around him,
Were deeply buried in sand.

You were in your 30s you said,
When the carnation revolution rose
Freedom restored in our land and others,
All buried branches, now on show.

# Roller Camera

Pig tails and the blue top
Standing on top of the stair case
Surrounded by your flower pots
Barely 6, but posing with grace

The Roller Camera was your idea
A way to freeze a moment in time
I was the first one to be photographed
So many, one or two would turn out fine

You took it with you when you travelled
Your roller camera, your other craft
But I can't tell you how happy it makes me
That I was the first one to be photographed.

# The Wardrobe

On the days you took me to work
I would get lost inside the wardrobe
It was a world of fear, of magic, of mess
A world beyond all those found in books.

Listening to your chats whilst with needle and
thread
You created magic, later seen on stage
Before becoming a part of this wardrobe's mess.

Masks, dresses, extravagant shoes and hats
The place led to no Narnia, but to a million other
worlds
That will forever be part of my childhood,
That will forever be part of my soul

Inside the wardrobe I could easily become
The wicked witch, the brave princess, the
fearsome clown-
I became all this and more in the space of a few
hours
But at the end of the day you would call my
name

And this is when you reminded me that above all
All I was, was your granddaughter,
And the luckiest child of all.

# You used to take me to ballet

You used to take me to ballet
Hover with me by the door
A world I earned to belong to
And you promised that one day I would.

You used to take me to ballet
Together, listening to the piano's prodding
You would allow me to dream and ask,
"Can you see, how they dance so gracefully?"

And promised that one day I would  too
Be part of this world of song, of wings and leaps
Of dreams I would have awake and not asleep
It was a promise that lived on, one that I held on

You used to take me to ballet
Any time before your atelier would open
We would both marvel at the grace, the magic,
The music, the art, the beauty

The songs that we hummed on the way
The dream I held on to,
 I wish you could still take me today.

# Wings

Grandma, do you remember,
Sunday mornings in pretty dresses
We stopped by the lake where they all gathered,
Their wings gleaming in the warming sun
The glistening waters greeting us like old
friends.

We would feed them leftover bread and biscuits
Which had grown hard with time
But for them it was the best meal
They would flap their wings in gratitude and
zeal.

You told me that all of us had wings,
That I had them too,
So if I wanted to fly
I could just do it, and I trusted you

You said that wings that try won't fall
Dreams are made of such things
Of kindness and belief
Take flight, get carried by the wind,
Let it lull you like an autumn leaf

The church bells tolling in the distance
Reminding us it was time to go
The walk smells of freshly baked bread and
coffee
Of Sunday strolls that meant so much
Of dreams I have dreamt and will forever hold
Of memories remembered until I grow old.

# Morning Storyteller

Stories are what comes to mind, when I think of
you
I have grown up loving them, but the best ones
have your voice
Stories, they would make me happy
Stories, they would make me cry
Stories that would scare me
And those that encouraged me to fly
Your voice, a remembered melody
Taking me in a warm embrace
A feeling so familiar, of comfort and home
cooked meals
Of stories that I believed in
Told from old, heavy books
Infinite portals to a world unknown
Or from the life you had lived
Early morning talks into warm coffee cups
Talks that made me forget those endless summer
months
For I will forever wish that they had indeed
never come to an end.

# The sound of my home

My home has a sound and it is the sound of your
laugh
Silver chuckle, music like a welcome knock on
the door
Warm and comforting, like the childhood
blanket you won't throw away;

My home has a smell and it is of your glycerine
soap
Of the eucalyptus sweets you used to share with
us
Of the old books you would read, of freshly
clean curtains in a spring breeze.

My home has a feeling and it is of your touch
Of your hand in mine and of your warm embrace
My home has a feeling and it is of you.

But above all my home has a sound,
And it is your laugh I hear when I walk through
the door
It tells me I'm home, it welcomes me in
And nothing reminds me more of home than
your own melody.

# Safety hook

Nothing would make us braver
Than the grip of your safety hook
Walks that smelt of spring and sea
You would encourage us to stop and look

But no matter what car drove past
What person walked by us
Your safety hook was a melody
That would always keep us close

Anytime we would go out
Walk down the streets of a familiar town
You would usher us along
With your safe, familiar grip

Now we walk these streets alone
No safety hook to bring us along
Tugging at our arm, a comforting touch
Grandma I wish you knew, it always meant so
much.

# Silhouette of a Seamstress

Whether they would come to you for your art
Or for your well-meaning advice
It was your name that came to mind
They wouldn't even think twice.

A grandmother, a friend, an artist
A loving voice, a patient ear
A hero, generous hand
With you there, there was nothing to fear

Morning walks through a busy town
Where your name would be heard
Through the streets that knew you so well
Your name was always preferred

Whether for a last minute alteration
Or years of well-planned designs
A need for a friendly phone call
Your laugh would always suffice

This island will forever know you
Forever hold your name dear
It is your art that will be remembered
And your memories forever sincere.

# Something missing

Goodbyes said outside your door
Hopes of a better future to hold
Letting go of what you gave
No one could have asked for more

So we take with us something to remember you
by
So much to leave behind
But you were my hardest goodbye

Overnight memories replaced by distant phone
calls
Cards that spoke of a missing love
A missed embrace, was it enough?

It never felt like it was.

# Your Lavender Perfume

I remember watching you, all those years ago
Needle in hand, always creating something new
You made me promises which made me smile
One day, when I was older, you would teach me
how to sew.

In those days you would tell me stories,
Of all the clothes you had made,
The wedding dresses, the prom suits
And all those with which I had played.

Summers will always smell of you
Of lavender perfume on your skin and closet
Of ginger bread and lemon tea
Of  vanilla biscuits and hot chocolate

Lavender days, lavender nights
How to forget such delights?
But when I went back, nothing was the same
You had forgotten my face, and couldn't
remember my name.

You could no longer bake,
Some of the dresses were unfinished
How to hold this needle? you asked
All the memories had diminished.

You have forgotten how to hold me,
And can't name those flowers in bloom
Grandma  but how could I forget
Your lavender perfume?

So if you have forgotten most
There is something I should say
I will keep it all close
Even what's been taken away
So even when all seems strange
Even when all you do is wrong
Know that my love hasn't changed
And you will find it in this song.

Oh grandma, your lavender perfume
Always so familiar, always so true
You have now forgotten most,
But please remember, I love you.

# Strange Monster

All those years ago
Grandma I heard you sing,
For the monster to go away
But now he is back, I think.

Late at night when I woke up
Your soothing voice would calm me down
You said you had searched everywhere
And it was nowhere to be found.

All those years ago
I feared the monster with the scary face
But you swore to always make sure
That he would never come to our place.

I believed you then,
And trustingly closed my eyes
Your arms would protect me
As I dreamed of blue skies.

Grandma, tonight he is here
And your voice can no longer be heard
He won't go away I fear
He won't listen to a word.

Once again whispering my name
It's him, it's undeniable
His voice no longer sounds the same
Although different, recognizable.

All those years ago,
Grandma I heard you sing
And now I wish you were still here
Hiding me under your wing.

# Memories that have thrived

Describing grandmother's home
Is describing a childhood we hold dear
Describing grandmother's home
Is describing a place with no fear

It is describing Christmas
With last minute decoration
It is remembering joyful tunes and dreams and
laugher
A place forever dear, kept safe in imagination

Describing grandmother's house
Is bringing back long summer days
Spent in front of the tiny TV and heavy books
that smelt old
Each story we were told, opening up a new
doorway

Describing grandmother's house
Is bringing back pretend play
A place where this felt real
Dreamy fabrics from your wardrobe, fresh
smelling flowers in May.

Grandma, your home smells of you.
It smells of lavender soap and all this is true.
Grandma, your home was also ours,
And if I could hold back the hours,
With all the things I have described
I would stop living through pen and paper
And live in the memories that have thrived.